B is for Battle Cry

A Civil War Alphabet

Written by Patricia Bauer and Illustrated by David Geister

*We have been looking forward to the time when we could dedicate
our first book together to our beloved parents:*

Ronald and Bernadine Bauer and David and Lucille Geister.

P. B. and D. G.

ACKNOWLEDGEMENTS

We extend our gratitude to the following historians who took the time to read and comment
on the manuscript: Stephen Osman, Charles Pautler, Aaron Novodvorsky, Spencer Johnson,
and Matthew Hutchinson. We are fortunate to call them friends.

A book like this one, with so many images, requires numerous models. We are very thankful
for the following friends, family members, and students who were kind enough to help us with
this project: Michael, Chris B., Taber, Kevin, Allie, Matthew, Dennis, Jerel, John, Jason, Eva, Andy,
Emma, Nathan, Ryan, Randy, Jeff, Erik, Keisha, Nicole, Chris, Maddie, Steve, and Vinnie.

Text Copyright © 2009 Patricia Bauer
Illustration Copyright © 2009 David Geister

Sleeping Bear Press®
310 North Main Street, Suite 300
Chelsea, MI 48118
www.sleepingbearpress.com

© 2009 Sleeping Bear Press is an imprint of Gale, a part of Cengage Learning.

Printed and bound in China.

First Edition

10 9 8 7 6 5 4 3 2 1

Library of Congress Cataloging-in-Publication Data

Bauer, Patricia.
B is for battle cry : a Civil War alphabet / written by Patricia Bauer ;
illustrated by David Geister.
p. cm.
Summary: "This alphabet shows an overview of the Civil War from A to Z.
Written in a two-tier format, a poem introduces the topic and detailed expository
text provides additional facts. Topics include Abraham Lincoln, Confederacy,
Emancipation Proclamation, Gettysburg, and Union"—Provided by publisher.
ISBN 978-1-58536-356-8
1. United States—History—Civil War, 1861-1865—Juvenile literature.
2. Alphabet books. I. Geister, David, ill. II. Title.
E468.9.B28 2009
973.7—dc22   2008040745

Author's Note

Mr. Lincoln's War, the War of Secession, the Brothers' War, the War Against Northern Aggression, the War for States' Rights, the War for Abolition … these are just a few of the names given to what Americans today call the Civil War (1861–1865).

As children, Dave (the illustrator and my husband) and I were both fascinated by the Civil War, and were greatly influenced by the books that we read. For Dave it was MacKinlay Kantor's *Gettysburg*, which his grandmother bought at a garage sale and read aloud to him when he was a young boy. I remember hiding Irene Hunt's *Across Five Aprils* under the supper table, trying to read and eat surrounded by my noisy brothers and sisters. Stories are what we as human beings are fascinated with, and these authors told stories that made us want to learn more. They showed us that history is so much more than facts and figures and dates.

This book is our way of introducing you to the Civil War. Our hope is that the words and paintings between the covers of this book will inspire you, the reader, to explore more stories of this war that occupies such a major place in the history of the United States.

Stephen Foster was a popular songwriter (which also makes him a storyteller) in the mid-nineteenth century, and one of his most famous songs is *Hard Times Come Again No More*. It is an especially appropriate song for the people who lived during the Civil War, who longed for a time when life would not be so difficult. Each poem in this book is written to fit into Foster's structure for the verses of the song, which means that the poems also work as a twenty-six-verse song.

A a

A is for Abraham Lincoln

He was called Honest Abe, the Rail Splitter, too,
but through the years he became so much more.
The boy who loved to read became the president who led
our country through the Civil War.

Abraham Lincoln, the sixteenth president of the United States, came from humble beginnings. He was born in a log cabin in Kentucky, on February 12, 1809, and didn't have much formal education. Lincoln's father, who was barely literate, discouraged his young son from learning. His mother died when he was nine years old and his father married a widow named Sarah Bush Johnson. She was not only kind and affectionate to Lincoln, but she encouraged him to learn.

Young Abe became known for his storytelling, which served him well as he grew older. Folks crowded around him as he made people laugh with his stories and jokes. This didn't sit well with his father, who broke up these gatherings so that young Lincoln could return to work. Though he gained a reputation for his strength, Abe had a great deal of ambition and realized at an early age that he didn't want to make his living doing manual labor.

As a young man, Lincoln was elected to the Illinois State Legislature and studied the law on his own. He wed Mary Todd and they eventually had four sons, though only two lived to adulthood. Lincoln was known for being an indulgent father, perhaps because of the loss of those sons.

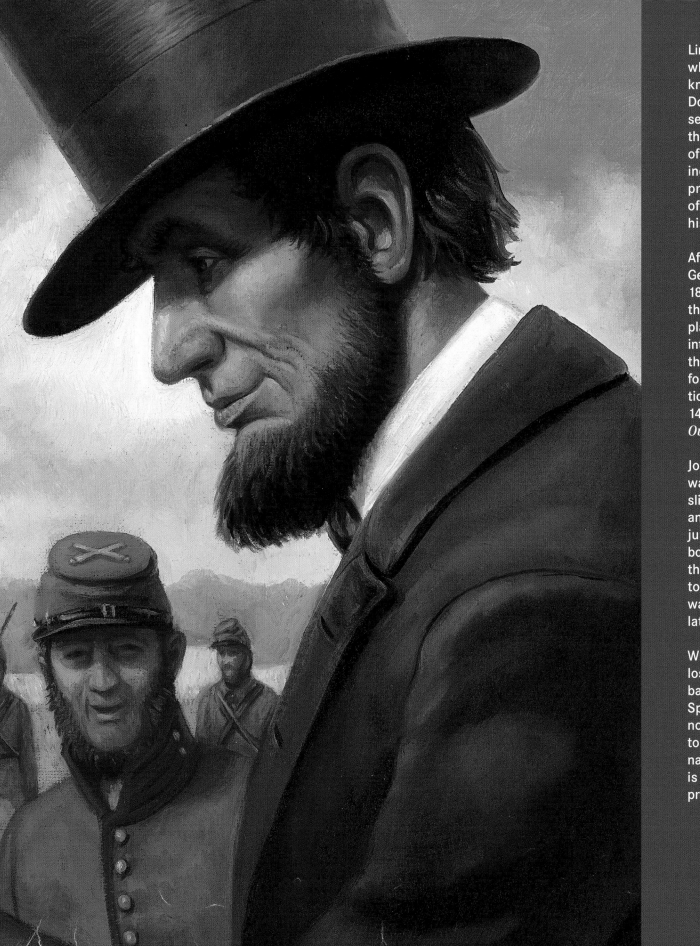

Lincoln's national reputation was set in 1858 when he exhibited great eloquence and knowledge during his debates with Stephen Douglas, his opponent for one of the senate seats from Illinois. Lincoln lost that race, but the stage was set for the presidential election of 1860, when he defeated Douglas. Though inexperienced, Lincoln proved to be a wise president who led the country during one of the most difficult times in America's history: the Civil War.

After four long years of fighting, Confederate General Robert E. Lee surrendered on April 9, 1865. President Lincoln's focus changed, from that of Commander in Chief of the army to planning the South's smooth transition back into the Union. (Union is a word that refers to the federal government, but also is the name for the North in the Civil War.) But a celebration was in order, and on the evening of April 14, the president took his wife to see the play *Our American Cousin* at Ford's Theatre.

John Wilkes Booth, a southern actor who was angry that the North had won the war, slipped into the Lincolns' box during the play and shot the president in the head. Then he jumped down onto the stage, breaking a bone in his leg, and yelled what many people think was *Sic Semper Tyrannis* ("As Always to Tyrants" in Latin). Booth escaped, but was later cornered in a barn and killed, in late April.

When Lincoln was assassinated, the country lost its champion for welcoming the South back into the nation. In his Second Inaugural Speech, Lincoln said, "With malice toward none; with charity for all . . . let us strive on to finish the work we are in; to bind up the nation's wounds . . ." Today Abraham Lincoln is considered by many to be the greatest president our country has ever known.

B is for Battles

Battles were fought in the North and in the South
at crossroads, creeks, and railroad towns.
Cannons fired and smoke filled up the air
as the soldiers charged across the ground.

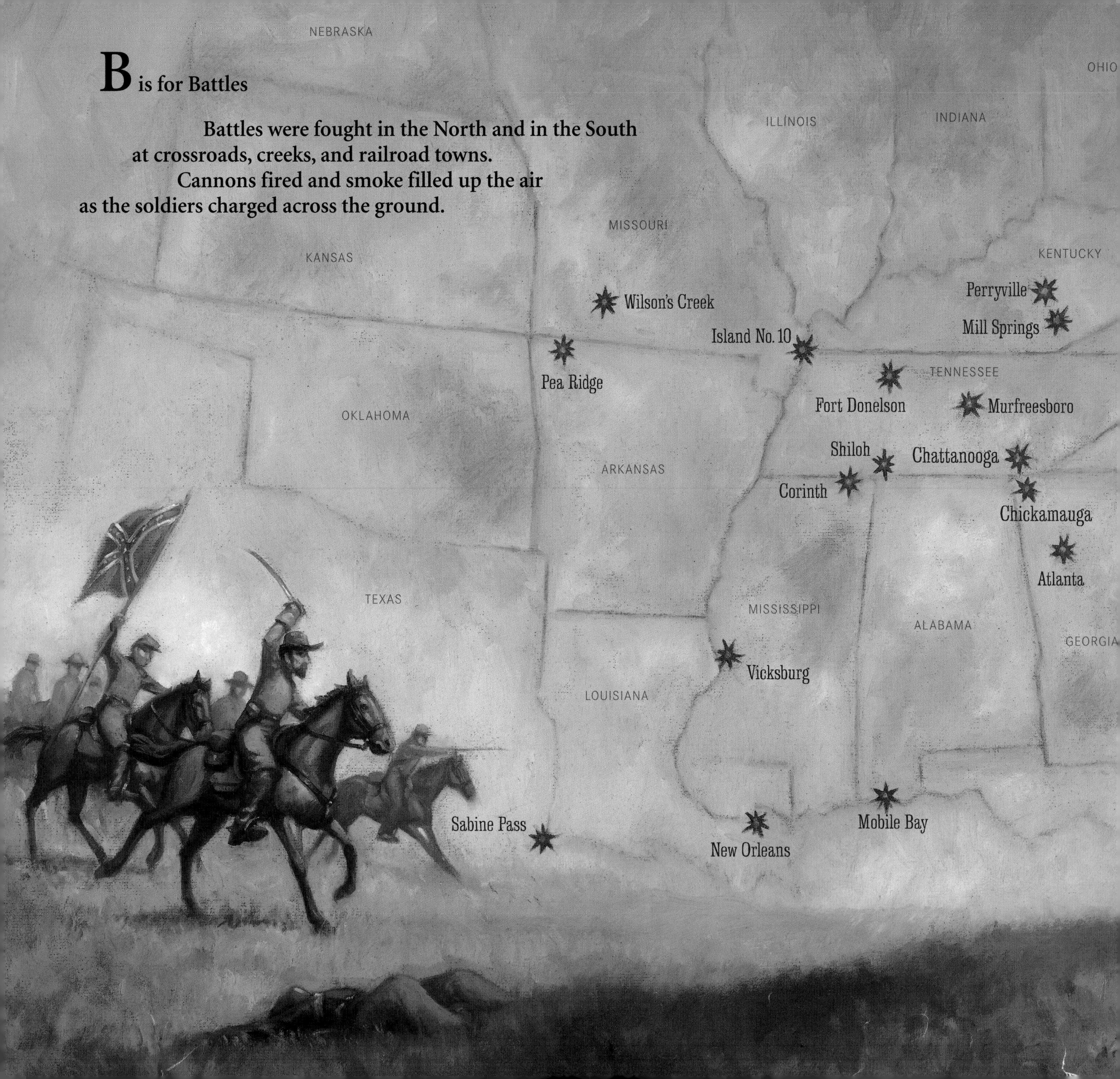

NEBRASKA

OHIO

ILLINOIS

INDIANA

MISSOURI

KANSAS

KENTUCKY

Perryville

Mill Springs

Wilson's Creek

Island No. 10

Pea Ridge

TENNESSEE

OKLAHOMA

Fort Donelson

Murfreesboro

Shiloh

Chattanooga

ARKANSAS

Corinth

Chickamauga

Atlanta

TEXAS

MISSISSIPPI

ALABAMA

GEORGIA

Vicksburg

LOUISIANA

Sabine Pass

New Orleans

Mobile Bay

Bb

Wars are made up of a series of battles. Thousands of battles and skirmishes were fought between the Confederate (Southern) and Union (Northern) forces during the Civil War. Gettysburg, Chickamauga, Bull Run, and Shiloh are a few of the most well known Civil War battles.

It is easy to be confused about names, however, because the same battle may have two different names. Northerners tended to name their battles after physical features of the land, while Southerners were more likely to name them after nearby villages, churches, or taverns. Thus, "Stones River" was named after a river, but the Southerners called it "Murfreesboro," after the village in Tennessee. "Bull Run" was named after the Virginia creek, but the Southerners referred to both Bull Run battles as "Manassas," after the railroad junction.

At the beginning of the war, men from both the South and the North rushed to enter the army before the fighting was over. Patriotism, glory, and adventure spurred many to join. Everyone was anxious to "see the elephant," the slang term for being in battle. That feeling changed for many of the soldiers once they experienced the horrible reality of battle.

Cc

Abraham Lincoln promised to keep slavery from spreading to new states and territories when he ran for president in 1860. That was enough for South Carolina to threaten that it would leave the United States if he were elected. In January of 1861, South Carolina did secede, or leave the Union, and the states of Alabama, Florida, Georgia, Louisiana, Mississippi, and Texas quickly followed.

The Civil War began when Fort Sumter, a federal (United States) fort off the coast of South Carolina, was fired upon by Confederate forces on April 12, 1861. Virginia, North Carolina, Arkansas, and Tennessee joined the new nation. Two other states, Kentucky and Missouri, were also counted, though they never officially seceded. These thirteen states made up the thirteen stars of the Confederate flag.

The issue of states' rights was central to the formation of the Confederacy. In other words, they believed that the state should be the highest authority, not the federal government. Some people even believed that each southern state should become a separate country. These beliefs sometimes made it difficult for the Confederacy to work together, as the states had different ideas about how to handle issues.

The Confederacy lasted only four years. When the capital of the Confederate states, Richmond, Virginia, fell to Union forces in early April of 1865, their dream of a new country died.

C is for Confederacy

The Southern Cross was the symbol for the states in the South known as the Confederacy.
Folks were loyal to their states and not the U.S.A., so they formed their own country.

At the time of the Civil War, the causes of most diseases were not understood. For instance, people believed that malaria was caused by miasmas (bad air), and not a parasite carried by mosquitoes, as we know today.

Whenever a large number of people come together, there is bound to be an increase in diseases. Many of the soldiers had grown up in isolated areas and hadn't contracted common childhood diseases like measles, mumps, and chicken pox, so these spread quickly among new recruits, causing many deaths.

Unsanitary conditions caused the vast majority of the illnesses. Decomposing food, garbage, and human and animal waste were often found within the camps, causing bacteria and viruses to spread. Countless deaths during the war were caused by intestinal diseases such as diarrhea, dysentery, and typhoid. Colds developed into pneumonia, killing many soldiers. Of those who died in the war, perhaps three of every five Union soldiers, and two of every three Confederate soldiers, died of disease.

Major Abraham Edward Welch expressed what many other soldiers may have felt as they were dying of disease. He wished that he could have died on the battlefield instead of in a sickbed.

D is for Diseases

Soldiers were sick with the measles and the pox—
illness struck many a courageous soul.
It wasn't only guns that killed the boys and men—
diseases took a mighty toll.

Slavery was the greatest moral and economic issue of pre-Civil War America. By the early nineteenth century, most slavery had disappeared from the North. However, the southern economy, based on large plantation crops like cotton and tobacco, continued to rely on slave labor.

Because of this, most southerners supported what was often called "the peculiar institution," even though the majority of southerners didn't own slaves. The North didn't want slavery to spread to new territories and states; the South wanted just the opposite. The rift between the North and South over the issue of slavery continued to grow and was one of the primary causes of the Civil War.

President Lincoln, who from a young age felt that slavery was evil, was a very skilled politician. Early in his presidency, he didn't believe that he had the political support to abolish slavery. But he came to the conclusion in the summer of 1862 that it was time to free the slaves, partly because he knew that the Confederates could not continue to win battles without the work of slaves. He wrote a draft of the Emancipation Proclamation over the course of several days, but his cabinet convinced him that it wouldn't be wise to make it public until there was a Union victory. Lincoln was not a popular president at this time and there were many in the North who did not want to see this become a war over slavery. While not a decisive victory, the battle of Antietam was enough of a victory that Lincoln felt that he could go public with the Emancipation Proclamation. Finally, on January 1, 1863, the president signed it into law.

E is for Emancipation Proclamation

Important words were written on paper by a man
who had this goal in mind—
sweet freedom for those who were slaves.
This document, Abe Lincoln did sign.

The Emancipation Proclamation freed the slaves only in the southern states, over which Lincoln had no control. So why was it important? It was the *idea* of freedom. "We shout for joy that we live to record this righteous decree," proclaimed the abolitionist and former slave, Frederick Douglass, who had denounced Lincoln earlier for not freeing the slaves. Southern slaves who heard the news were given hope. Some ran away, knowing that they would be free if they joined up with the Union army.

Lincoln also proclaimed that former slaves would be accepted into the service of the Union. These soldiers of the United States Colored Troops, of which the 54th Massachusetts Regiment is the most famous, fought valiantly for their freedom and the Union cause. By the end of the war, approximately ten percent of the Union army (about 180,000 men) was made up of black soldiers.

Ee

Abraham Lincoln was inaugurated on March 4, 1861. Not long after, the first act of the war occurred in the early morning hours of April 12, in South Carolina's Charleston Harbor. Fort Sumter, a federal fort, was located on an island off the coast. Many southerners looked upon the fort as a symbol of northern aggression and didn't want it there.

The Confederates demanded that the federal troops surrender. When they didn't, General Beauregard ordered his artillery (cannons) to fire on the fort. The battle lasted for thirty-four hours before the Union troops ran out of supplies and were forced to surrender. Charleston Harbor was controlled by the Confederacy for the rest of the war.

On April 14, 1865, Major General Anderson, who surrendered the fort exactly four years earlier, raised the same American flag triumphantly over Fort Sumter at the end of the war.

F is for Fort Sumter

The war began in April of 1861
    when shells hit Fort Sumter before dawn.
The fort was short of ammunition, men, and supplies
    and soon the Union soldiers were gone.

Gg

G is for Gettysburg

A three-day battle was fought at Gettysburg,
in Pennsylvania; it was a small town.
Thousands of soldiers fell during the fight
and are buried in that hallowed ground.

In 1863, Gettysburg, Pennsylvania, was a quiet town nestled in rolling hills, with a population of about 2,400 people. It was a transportation hub, which is one of the reasons that the battle was fought there.

General Robert E. Lee intended to take the fighting to the North, out of Virginia, where it had been disrupting agriculture and daily life for two years. There would be more food available for his men to forage (find or steal), and he hoped to disrupt communications and supplies to Washington and Baltimore. He knew that if he could win battles in the North, it would be good for the morale of the Confederacy.

The battle began on July 1 and continued for two more days, with many brave men falling on both sides. Places like Little Round Top, Cemetery Ridge, the Wheat Field, and the Peach Orchard became the sites of battles, drenched in blood. Pickett's Charge, led by Confederate General George Pickett, was the most infamous assault of the battle. This three-day slaughter left more casualties than any other battle in American history; the combined total for North and South was more than 50,000. Surviving soldiers, along with civilians, hastily buried the dead in shallow graves. Within a few months, some of these graves were uncovered by wind and rain. The need for more permanent resting places was obvious. On November 19, 1863, ten thousand people came to witness the dedication of the cemetery at Gettysburg.

Edward Everett, a well-known orator, was the main speaker. President Lincoln, whose popularity was low at that time, was invited as a formality. Upon their arrival, it was obvious that a terrible battle had been fought, as there were scarred trees, scraps of clothing, broken fences, and artillery pieces scattered across the hills. The smell of decomposing horses still wafted through the air. After Everett's two-hour speech ended, receiving thunderous applause, it was the president's turn. His speech lasted about two minutes, and people who were further back in the crowd didn't even realize that he had started. His speech began, "Fourscore and seven years ago our fathers brought forth upon this continent, a new nation, conceived in Liberty, and dedicated to the proposition that all men are created equal." Those are the first words in one of the most important speeches in American history.

H is for Hardtack

Rations of hardtack, crackers hard as rocks,
the soldiers would often break them up.
They'd dunk them in their coffee, or stir them in their soup,
sometimes weevils floated to the top.

Hardtack, beans, hardtack, meat, parched corn, and more hardtack. Soldiers survived on a monotonous diet. Each Union soldier received about ten pieces of hardtack (thick crackers made of flour, water, and salt) as part of their daily rations. Confederates, often on shorter rations, received fewer. Hardtack was often broken up into coffee or soup. Weevils (bugs) would float to the surface of the liquid, and the soldiers became accustomed to skimming them off. Broken pieces of hardtack were fried in fat to make a dish called skillygalee.

Southern soldiers combined cornmeal with lard, water, and an egg (if one was to be found), making corndodgers, a type of cornbread. Another southern staple was cornmeal or flour mixed with bacon fat and fried together, making a "delicacy" called sloosh.

Soldiers supplemented their rations by foraging for food. If they had a bit of extra money, they might buy from local civilians or from the sutler (storekeeper who traveled with the army). They also looked forward to packages from home that contained treats such as jam, sardines, and cakes. Young men, notorious for always being hungry, tried to fill their bellies whenever and however they could.

Hh

I is for Ironclads

Sailors fought in wooden ships for many centuries
until the Civil War
when iron was placed on the outside of the hull
and the ironclad ship was born.

Ii

The Civil War is known for great technological innovations that permanently changed warfare. One of these was the invention of the ironclad ship. Up until 1862 ships were made of wood. From that time on, the wooden ships would be clad, or covered, with metal.

The Confederate navy built a new ironclad ship to defend its ports from Union attack. They used the burned-out hull of a Union ship, the USS *Merrimack*, as an understructure and renamed it the CSS *Virginia*. However, the ship is generally referred to by its original name.

On its first encounter, at Hampton Roads in Virginia, near where the James River flows into the Chesapeake Bay, the *Virginia* easily destroyed the Union's wooden ships. The Union's cannonballs bounced off the sides of the *Virginia*. As night descended, the captain of the *Virginia* steered the ship to safe harbor, confident that they would return the next day and destroy the rest of the Union fleet. What the captain didn't know is that during the night, the Union navy's newly built ironclad ship, the *Monitor*, arrived in the harbor.

The two ships fought each other for four hours, while thousands of spectators watched from shore. Finally, the *Monitor* was hit in its pilothouse, injuring the captain. While the command changed, the *Virginia* sailed away. Both sides claimed victory in a battle that neither side won.

Like Abraham Lincoln, Jefferson Davis was born in Kentucky. In fact, they were born within a year of each other. Davis was born in 1808 and Lincoln in 1809. While Davis still was a baby his father moved the family to Mississippi, where he would spend a great deal of his life. He once told his father that he didn't want to attend school, so his father told him that he would have to work in the fields. After two days of this, "Little Jeff" decided that he preferred school!

At the age of sixteen, Jefferson entered the U.S. Military Academy at West Point. He found that he enjoyed the military life. He served in the army on the frontier during the Black Hawk War in 1832, as did Lincoln. His skill and bravery as an officer in the Mexican War (1846-48) brought him much praise. Davis also served as a U.S. Senator from Mississippi as well as the Secretary of War in the cabinet of the fourteenth president, Franklin Pierce.

Jefferson Davis accepted the position of President of the Confederacy because he believed passionately that the South had the right to secede from the United States. He served from 1861-1865, and was the only president of the Confederate States of America.

Jj

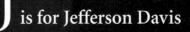

J is for Jefferson Davis

Jefferson Davis was the only president
of the Confederate States.
He led his new country in a war against the North
till the surrender on that April day.

Kk

Johnny Reb and Billy Yank, slang terms for southern and northern soldiers, wore many different hats throughout the war. Kepis were caps with low circular crowns and small visors, modeled on French military caps. The forage cap looked a lot like a kepi, but was taller and not as rigid. Many soldiers preferred the soft-brimmed slouch hats because they kept the sun and rain out of their eyes. Some wore the more formal Hardee hat, which had a brim and a tall crown, but many soldiers complained that it was heavy and hot.

At the beginning of the war, it was difficult to distinguish between the northern and southern soldiers. Many of the uniforms were provided by individual states or towns, which made it extremely confusing. Early in the war, at the Battle of Bull Run/Manassas, the 2nd Wisconsin Infantry wore state issued gray uniforms and were fired upon by their own side. Some members of the 5th Virginia Infantry wore blue uniforms in the same battle, which caused confusion.

Eventually, blue became the standard uniform color for the Union, while most Confederate soldiers wore gray or butternut (a light brown color made from butternut hulls). A typical Union soldier wore a loose-fitting, four-button sack coat, while Confederate soldiers usually wore short gray shell jackets.

K is for Kepi

Men wore kepis perched upon their heads.
Soldiers wore them in rain or shine.
Whether they were from the North or from the South,
the men looked like soldiers so fine.

L is for Letters

Dearest Papa, we wish that you were home—
we miss you more than words can say.
   Mama's helping me to spell and she sends her love.
We pray you'll walk through the door someday.

Love letters, business letters, letters filled with joy and grief ... all of these and many more circulated throughout the country during the war. Soldiers, writing by the light of a candle stub, or perhaps at a roadside on the march, put their thoughts on paper. Some could barely spell; others wrote with great eloquence and beauty. The girls who were left behind sometimes wrote to their sweethearts from their schoolrooms, or between shifts in a munitions factory. Women wrote of their new babies, born since their husbands went away, as well as the deaths of beloved family members. Children practiced their new skills by writing letters to their fathers and brothers. Families gathered together to read the precious letters their soldiers sent from far away.

Soldiers waited anxiously to receive word from their families and friends, and many expressed sadness or frustration when they didn't receive letters as frequently as they would have liked. Civilians and soldiers labored over letters that might take weeks or months to reach their destinations. So much of what is known about life during the Civil War is because of letters that, thankfully, were preserved.

Ll

Music played an integral role in soldiers' lives. The loud field drum kept them in step as they marched. The fife (a high-pitched flute) signaled when it was time to get up, go to sleep, and eat. Many of the musicians were young boys who were supposed to be at least twelve years old. But some, like Avery Brown of Ohio, who was not quite nine, managed to enlist and serve out the war. Many Confederate and Union regiments had their own bands, which served as important morale builders during difficult times.

Singing was a form of entertainment that didn't require any extra equipment. The average person in the nineteenth century knew the lyrics and tunes to many songs and could entertain themselves and others for hours. Imagine a group of soldiers sitting around a campfire in the dark, when someone starts to sing a sentimental ballad like "Aura Lee," and soon everyone joins in. Each man conjures up a different image of life back home. It doesn't matter whether the soldier is wearing blue or gray; he feels a melancholy tug at his heart as the lyrics hang in the air.

M m

M is for Music

Soldiers marched to the beat of the fife and the drum,
or whistled as they stood in line.
Some had tears in their eyes as they sang of home sweet home,
and the girls that they had left behind.

N n

Women served as nurses in the Civil War, angels of the battlefield.
They cared for the sick and the wounded men—their skills helped the soldiers heal.

Early in the war, Dorothea Dix was appointed superintendent of nurses for the Union army. Her rules didn't allow young or pretty women in the Nurse Corps and restricted what they wore to somber clothes with no jewelry or hoopskirts. In the mid-nineteenth century, nursing was not considered a respectable occupation for women, and Miss Dix wanted to be sure that only serious women who weren't looking for husbands became nurses. Thousands served for both sides and proved that women could handle the difficult work of wartime nursing, though men continued to dominate the profession.

Clara Barton was very successful at raising money and supplies, and worked independently from the official army nurses corps. She was on the front lines in a number of battles, including Antietam, where she was so close to the lines that a minie ball went through her sleeve and killed the man she was attending. The writers Walt Whitman and Louisa May Alcott both wrote about their experiences as nurses during the war.

The nurse took the place of mother, wife, or sister for many a stricken soldier as he lay sick or dying. Soldiers who survived often felt that they owed a great debt to the nurses who attended them.

The military is built upon a hierarchy. Even though a civilian, the president acts as the commander in chief. During the Civil War, Jefferson Davis was in that position for the Confederacy and Abraham Lincoln for the Union.

Officers receive their commissions from Congress. The highest-ranking military office in the army is general. Around a thousand men served as generals for both sides during the Civil War. Ulysses S. Grant became the most well known general for the North. Other important Union generals were George McClellan, Winfield Scott Hancock, and William Sherman. The Confederacy's most important general was Robert E. Lee. Others who gained fame were Thomas "Stonewall" Jackson (who held his position like a "stone wall" at the first Battle of Bull Run/Manassas), Joseph Johnston, and John B. Gordon. Officers in the army were in command of the infantry (foot soldiers), cavalry (soldiers on horseback), and artillery (soldiers in charge of firing the large weapons such as cannons).

The navy's officers commanded sailors on ships. David Farragut was the first man to serve as an admiral, the highest rank in the navy. Admiral Raphael Semmes resigned his position with the federal government to become the commander of the Confederate navy.

O is for Officers

Officers gave orders to all the men.
They told the soldiers when to fire.
Captains, majors, and generals, too,
the best ones were loved and admired.

P is for Prisoners of War

Many a soldiers from the North and from the South
were taken as prisoners of war.
Some were kept in confinement, others were exchanged,
but many died before peace was restored.

During battle, soldiers who escape death often are captured and become prisoners of war. In the beginning of the Civil War, these prisoners were usually exchanged with the enemy. For instance, a Confederate private (the lowest rank) was exchanged evenly for a Union private, or a general could be exchanged for forty-six privates! By 1863, both sides held many prisoners in camps scattered throughout the North and South.

One of these prisons was located in Elmira, New York, and over 12,000 Confederate prisoners were eventually confined there. Conditions were horrible. There was no clean water, the winter cold was especially harsh on men who were accustomed to a warmer climate, and vegetables were in short supply, which meant that many men contracted scurvy. One-fourth of the prisoners died, giving Elmira the highest death rate of any northern prisoner of war camp.

The most notorious camp was Andersonville, Georgia, where many of the same conditions existed as at Elmira, though instead of cold, the heat was horrendous. Disease spread through the overcrowded camp and there was little food. When the camp was liberated, many of the prisoners looked like skeletons. Over thirty percent of the approximately 45,000 prisoners died in captivity.

Q is for Quartermaster

The quartermaster's job was to supply the army's needs.
Wagons traveled many miles over the ground
taking rations to the soldiers and hay for the mules.
And ammunition was hauled around.

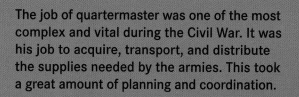

The job of quartermaster was one of the most complex and vital during the Civil War. It was his job to acquire, transport, and distribute the supplies needed by the armies. This took a great amount of planning and coordination.

While the army's Subsistence Department supplied the rations for the troops, the Quartermaster Department inspected, packed, and transported the rations to the soldiers. An army traveled with supply wagons organized as "trains." The men who drove them were called teamsters. Wagons were loaded with food, medical supplies, and ammunition. These were pulled by mules and stretched for miles behind the soldiers. Railroad trains and boats also carried supplies.

Quartermasters were often called upon to be creative in order to supply the troops. When a railroad bridge over the Tennessee River was destroyed, General William LeDuc had his men improvise a crude steamboat to carry rations to the Union troops at Chattanooga, who were almost out of food. Southern quartermasters had an especially difficult time providing for their troops, as there wasn't an efficient system in place for transporting the goods that were available. Uniforms, shoes, and food were all in short supply.

Rr

Yelling like demons, Rebels went on the attack,
striking terror in the enemy's eyes.
Hollering, whooping, and shouting through the ranks—
the southern soldiers shrieked out their cries.

A company of Yankee soldiers waits nervously for their orders to attack the enemy. The officer barks at them to advance, but as they do, their ears are greeted with a high-pitched, savage scream that seems to travel through their bones, causing them to hesitate for just a moment. That scream has often been referred to as the Rebel yell, a screech that showed their individual and collective strength and determination and was meant to intimidate the enemy. And it usually had that effect, especially when thousands of Rebels yelled at the same time.

The Union soldiers also had a distinctive yell, but it was much deeper, more like a "hurrah." It didn't seem to have that same ability to strike fear in the enemy.

The Rebel yell, which once caused terror to ripple through the Yankee ranks, is lost to us today. There are written descriptions and several possible recordings of elderly Confederate veterans, but we are mostly left to use our imaginations to transport us back to Manassas or Chickamauga or countless other fields of battle where the echoes of the yell may still be carried on the wind.

There were many daring people who served as spies during the war, including countless women and blacks. Women were not generally thought of as being treacherous, and many men of the time didn't credit them with being intelligent. Escaped slaves and free blacks often made the best spies, having developed these survival skills in order to find out information without being seen or heard.

Rose O'Neale Greenhow was a Washington society hostess who became one of the most notorious southern spies. She was captured and imprisoned, but after her release she traveled to Europe. Upon her return, her ship encountered a blockade. Mrs. Greenhow tried to escape in a rowboat, but it capsized and she drowned, partly due to the weight of the gold she had acquired from English supporters.

Harriet Tubman, the celebrated "conductor" of the Underground Railroad, served as a scout, nurse, and spy during the war. She also organized an information-gathering network of blacks for the Union army in South Carolina.

The Dabneys were a black husband-and-wife spy team. Mrs. Dabney put herself in danger by going south to work as a laundress. She and her husband employed a series of signals using clothes hung up on the line to communicate the movements of the Confederates.

S s

S is for Spies

Wild Rose was a lady who spied for the South.
There were more who also did the same.
Harriet Tubman passed information to the North—
many others, we'll never know their names.

The Civil War has often been called the first modern war, for good reason. Recent inventions such as the telegraph, photography, and railroads were employed by both the South and the North. Advances in weaponry also forced changes in tactics, making this a new type of war.

President Lincoln encouraged new technology. He was the first president to use telegrams (messages sent through wires) to communicate with his officers and to stay aware of what was happening on the battlefields. Wherever the armies traveled, telegraph wires appeared. The lightning speed of the telegraph allowed news to travel much more quickly than written messages.

Moving troops and supplies by railroad became an important military strategy. Many battles were fought at railroad centers such as Manassas Junction. The course of more than one battle was changed as a result of the arrival of fresh troops by train.

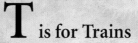

T is for Trains

Trains carried soldiers to the battlefields.
Tracks crisscrossed the South and the North.
Telegraph wires stretched across the land,
and messages were sent back and forth.

Tt

New weapons technology changed the face of war. A new type of bullet, called the minie ball, was a great improvement over the round ball that was used in the earlier muskets (guns). Minie balls could be loaded quickly into rifles, which had grooves inside the barrels, making the weapon more accurate than the smoothbore muskets. Another breakthrough was the invention of breech-loading rifles, which were easier and quicker to load and fire.

Rifled cannons, which were more accurate and had a longer range than their smoothbore counterparts, also made their appearance during the Civil War. Several rapid-fire guns, like the Gatling gun invented during the war, could be called predecessors to the machine gun.

The Confederates experimented with a submarine, called the CSS *Hunley*. It successfully sunk a ship in Charleston Harbor, but it sank shortly afterwards with its entire crew. Similar experiments occurred in the North, where a submarine called the "Intelligent Whale" was developed, but the war ended and it never saw action. Both the Union and the Confederacy attempted to develop hot air balloons to gather information, but neither side was very successful in their attempts.

Photographers such as Mathew Brady brought the war home. For the first time, images of battlefields and death were available to those who weren't on the field. Photography also allowed soldiers to carry pictures of their loved ones on their marches and into their battles. For those soldiers who died, their heroic images on tin or glass were all that remained of them at the end of the war.

U is for Union

The Union was made up of the northern states—
there were twenty-three in all.
The soldiers fought to keep their country as one,
and after four years the South did fall.

The definition of "union" is to join two or more things into one. The United States is a union of individual states that have come together and act as one. Each state has its own government and individual "personality," but the federal government has power over all of them. The northern states were referred to as the Union because they remained loyal to the existing federal government, the old Union.

President Lincoln stated very clearly that the war was to preserve the Union. In the beginning, he tried to distance that goal from that of freeing the slaves because he knew that emancipation was an unpopular idea and he didn't have the political power to make that change. However, by 1862, he wrote the Emancipation Proclamation, which made it clear that the war was now also about slavery.

Today, as a result of the Civil War and Reconstruction (the time following the war), we are one union again, the United States, not two countries opposed to each other.

By the autumn of 1862, the Union army took control of the entire Mississippi River except for Vicksburg, Mississippi. If the federal forces could take the city, it would mean that the Confederacy wouldn't be able to use the river to move troops and supplies.

By the spring of 1863, General Grant decided that a siege would be the best strategy. This meant that Grant's army would surround the city, not allowing people or supplies in or out, in an attempt to capture it. Many citizens of Vicksburg dug caves into the hillsides and lived there to escape the bombardment of Union artillery. In order to stave off starvation, soldiers and civilians ate mules, horses, cats, dogs, rats, and mice. Boredom was another problem, and there are accounts of the enemies conversing and singing with each other.

The siege ended on July 4, 1863, with the surrender of Vicksburg. This occurred on the day after the battle of Gettysburg, which meant that there were two devastating Confederate losses, one in the West and one in the East, at virtually the same time.

V v

V is for Vicksburg

Vicksburg families huddled inside caves—
shells were bursting and starvation was near.
The Union army had put the city under siege.
For many weeks the people lived in fear.

During times of war, women have successfully ventured out of their traditional roles, and those who lived during the Civil War were no exception. Many women in the North went to work in factories, some of them performing dangerous work making cartridges to supply the soldiers with ammunition. Women on both sides were left to manage farms and plantations and do the hard physical labor involved in growing crops. They did all of this in addition to raising and caring for their families.

Dr. Elizabeth Blackwell formed an organization to collect and distribute medical supplies, and also set up a training course for nurses. Dr. Mary Edwards Walker, after first being denied the right to serve as a doctor, was granted the post of assistant surgeon. She served in a number of capacities (including spy) before she was taken prisoner. Dr. Walker is still the only woman in history to receive the Congressional Medal of Honor.

There were a number of women who disguised themselves as men and served in the army. Frances Clalin and Sarah Edmonds are two of the most famous Union soldiers, while Loreta Valazquez and Amy Clark served in the Confederate Army. There may have been hundreds of women who served as soldiers, but their names and stories will never be known.

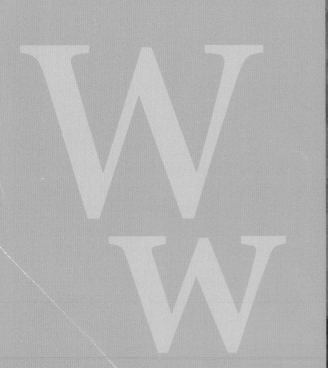

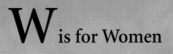 W is for Women

Some disguised themselves as soldiers and fought beside the men.
Some stayed home and worked upon the farms.
Others nursed the sick and wounded and scrounged for supplies.
They tried to keep their families safe from harm.

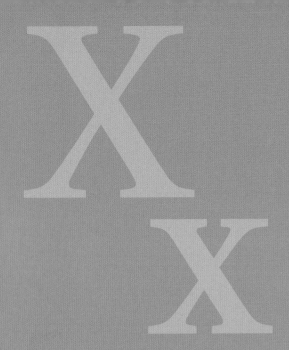

X x

The war had dragged on for four long years, with a devastating effect on both the North and South. After the capture of the Confederate capital of Richmond, Grant's army blocked General Lee's retreating army near Appomattox Court House, Virginia. The Confederates had exhausted all of their strength and resources. Faced with no other options and wanting to preserve the lives of his remaining men, General Lee surrendered.

Lee, wearing his finest dress uniform, arrived first at Wilbur McLean's home, where negotiations would take place. Grant had just come off the field, and when he made his appearance, he was dressed in what he called "rough garb" with no sash or sword, and only his shoulder straps to show his rank. Their meeting was a formal and solemn occasion.

The terms of surrender were very generous. Grant allowed the Confederate soldiers to take their horses and mules because it was planting time and those animals would be needed in the fields. The southern soldiers were starving, and Grant made sure they had rations, not just for the day, but for their journey home. When a band began to play in celebration and the Union soldiers started to cheer, General Grant made them stop and said, "The war is over. The Rebels are our countrymen again."

X is for AppomattoX

The Civil War battles lasted four long years.
        The Rebel soldiers had empty haversacks.
    General Lee surrendered to General Grant
            in a village called Appomattox.

Yy

Y is for Yankee

A Yankee was a soldier who fought for the North,
to preserve his country was his goal.
His president was Lincoln, who wanted all to be free.
The Yanks won, but it took a mighty toll.

Yankee is a name that was common long before the Civil War (think of the song "Yankee Doodle" from the Revolutionary War) and referred to people who lived in the colonies, and later, the United States. It particularly referred to the inhabitants of New England, and still does today.

During the Civil War, the name came to be applied to those who were loyal to the Union. "Billy Yank" was the nickname given to a Union soldier, regardless of the northern state from which he originated. Most Yankee sympathizers lived north of the Mason-Dixon line, which was established during colonial times, but there were some in the South, as well.

Confederates were also referred to as rebels because they were rebelling against the established United States government. Thus, the name given to Confederate soldiers was "Johnny Reb." They generally lived south of the Mason-Dixon line.

All too often, brothers, cousins, and friends found themselves on opposite sides in the war. President Lincoln's wife, Mary, had a brother and several half-brothers, as well as other relatives, who were Confederate soldiers. This is why the war is sometimes called "The Brothers' War."

Many states, both North and South, raised Zouave (zoo-AHV) units during the Civil War. The soldiers adopted the name and the distinctive uniforms from African units that had fought with the French in North Africa during the 1830s. Their uniforms consisted of baggy trousers, a short jacket, and a fez or turban. This exotic clothing was in stark contrast to the regular uniforms that most soldiers wore. Zouaves became known for their dashing military exercises and drills.

Elmer Ellsworth, a colonel in the Union army, is credited with starting the Zouave movement in the United States. Colonel Ellsworth raised the First Regiment of Fire Zouaves, made up of men he recruited from the New York Fire Department. He was shot after pulling down a Confederate flag from a hotel in Alexandria, Virginia, and is thought to be the first Union officer killed in the war.

Though the Union had many more Zouave units, the Confederates also raised Zouaves. One of the most notable was Coppens' 1st Battalion of Louisiana Zouaves. Many of the men spoke French and the battalion served out most of the war in Virginia. They fought valiantly at the Battle of Antietam/ Sharpsburg, where their unit was almost wiped out.

Zz

Z is for Zouaves

Some had jackets trimmed in yellow, and baggy red pants.
These brightly dressed soldiers had a name—
Zouaves, they were called, in the North and in the South,
and in the end, they gained great fame.

Glossary

Abolitionist: someone who wants to abolish, or get rid of slavery

Black Hawk War: a war fought in 1832 in the Midwest between Native Americans, settlers, and the U.S. Army. It was named after Chief Black Hawk, who led the Sac and Fox people in this fight over land.

Blockade: an effort to prevent supplies, troops, information, or aid from reaching the enemy

Breech-loading: a gun that is loaded at the breech, or rear, of the barrel

Cartridge: ammunition that is fired from a gun. In the Civil War, this usually consisted of black powder and a minie ball tied in paper.

Civilian: anyone not in the military

Commission: a specific order granting a person the rank of officer

Corps: a military unit that specializes in a certain task, such as the medical corps. It is also a large unit in the army, consisting of several thousand soldiers.

Fourscore: A score is twenty years, so fourscore is eighty years.

Haversack: a bag for carrying rations and other belongings of a soldier

Hierarchy: a system of ranking or ordering things or people

Inauguration: the ceremony when the new president takes office

Liberty: freedom

Mason-Dixon Line: a survey line that originated before the Revolutionary War, but became known as the dividing line between the North and South during the Civil War

Mexican War: a war that began in 1846 over Texas lands. It ended in 1848 with the U.S. acquiring new lands from Mexico in the Southwest.

Minie ball: a lead bullet that was often used in the Civil War. It was named after its French inventor, Claude-Étienne Minié.

Morale: the spirit of a person; how she or he is feeling

Musket: a common gun used during the Civil War that was loaded through the muzzle, or front end of the barrel

Orator: a great speaker

Patriotism: love of one's country

Peculiar Institution: a term used for slavery

Port: a place where ships can load and unload people and goods

Rail Splitter: This was Abraham Lincoln's nickname because he was a woodsman who was known for his strength, especially for splitting logs to build fences.

Ration: a specific amount of food; soldiers received daily rations

Regiment: a military unit. In the Civil War a regiment numbered approximately 1,000 soldiers.

Scurvy: a disease caused by lack of vitamin C

Skirmish: a minor, or small battle

Tactics: specific deployment or movement of soldiers on the battlefield

Underground Railroad: a secret network of people and places that helped slaves escape to the North

This book belongs to

To weather watchers
and cloud spotters

Thank you to
Kallie George
and meteorologist
Phil Chadwick

Tundra Books, an imprint of Penguin Random House Canada
Young Readers, a Penguin Random House Company

Library and Archives Canada Cataloguing in Publication
MacKay, Elly, author, illustrator
        Red sky at night / Elly MacKay.
Issued in print and electronic formats.
ISBN 978-1-101-91783-1 (hardcover).—ISBN 978-1-101-91785-5
(EPUB)
        I. Title.
PS8625.K38845R43 2018   jC813'.6
C2017-902902-9   C2017-902903-7

Published simultaneously in the United States of America by
Tundra Books of Northern New York, an imprint of Penguin
Random House Canada Young Readers, a Penguin Random
House Company

Library of Congress Control Number: 2017940264

Edited by Tara Walker
Designed by Kelly Hill
The illustrations in this book are photographs of paper dioramas.
The text was set in Yana.
Printed and bound in China
www.penguinrandomhouse.ca

1 2 3 4 5   22 21 20 19 18

Penguin
Random House
tundra | TUNDRA BOOKS

SOURCES

Books

Bowen, David. *Weather Lore — Guide to Weather Quotes,
Sayings and Proverbs*. Hob Hill Books, 2013. eBook.

Day, Cindy. *Grandma Says: Weather Lore from Meteorologist
Cindy Day*. Halifax, NS: Nimbus, 2013. Print.

Lalonde, Shirley. *Never Sell Your Hen on a Rainy Day: Weather
Signs, Rhymes and Reasons*. Kelowna, B.C.: Sandhill, 1998. Print.

Stackpole Books, eds. *Survival Wisdom and Know-How*. New
York, NY: Black Dog & Leventhal, 2007. Print.

Websites

Environment and Climate Change Canada:
Sky Watchers' Guide
https://ec.gc.ca/meteoaloeil-skywatchers/

The Old Farmer's Almanac
https://www.almanac.com

Royal Meteorological Society
http://www.metlink.org

UCAR Center for Science Education
https://scied.ucar.edu/webweather

RED SKY AT NIGHT

ELLY MacKAY

tundra

WEATHER FOLKLORE

Long ago, here and far away, people looked for clues in nature to predict the weather. They learned from experience by watching the shapes of clouds or noticing the behavior of animals. This wisdom was passed down through sayings like the ones in this book.

How weather-wise are you?

Might you know a saying or two?

Red sky at night, sailor's delight.

When the dew is on the grass,
no rain will come to pass.

Evening red and morning gray,
two sure signs of one fine day.

When the mist creeps up the hill,
fishers, it's time to try your skill.

No weather is ill if the wind be still.

If woolly fleeces are in the sky,
be sure the day is fine and dry.

When ladybugs swarm, expect a day that's warm.

When the wind is from the West,
then the fishes bite the best.

Yellow streaks in a sunset sky,
wind and daylong rain are nigh.

Frogs will call before the rain,
but in the sun are quiet again.

Whether it's cold or whether it's hot,
we shall have weather, whether or not.

Ring around the moon, rain will come soon.

Red sky in the morning, sailors take warning!

Trout jump high when rain is nigh.

Hear the whistle of the train?

'Tis a sign it's going to rain.

Winds of the daytime wrestle and fight,
longer and stronger than those of the night.

Wind from the East
is neither good for man nor beast.

Little ships must keep to shore.
Larger ships may venture more.

If seabirds fly to land,
there truly is a storm at hand.

When clouds appear like rocks and towers,
the Earth is refreshed with frequent showers.

Cats leap about and chase their tails
to warn of thunderstorms and gales.

When the forest murmurs and the mountain roars,
close the windows and shut the doors!

The more rain, the more rest.
Fair weather's not always best.

Now that you know a saying or two,

can you predict what the weather will do?

WEATHER WISDOM

Weather sayings have deep roots. Before people could check a weather report, they kept a close eye on the sky and watched the behavior of animals to predict approaching storms. Reading the skies meant they could bring a boat back to land or take animals to a safe place before the weather changed. There are many versions of these sayings. Some sayings in this book have been updated in order to be passed on to younger generations, though the messages remain the same. Their accuracy may vary depending on season or location, but all are based on observations from nature and share valuable weather wisdom and a connection to the past.

Red sky at night, sailor's delight.
True (in temperate zones). In some parts of the world, the saying goes, "Red sky at night, shepherd's delight." But whether you are on the sea or in the meadow, red skies (but not red clouds) at sunset mean there is calm air in the western sky. By the next morning, that nice weather should be right overhead.

When the dew is on the grass, no rain will come to pass.
Usually true. If there is dew, it means there was a clear sky throughout the night. Of course, it doesn't tell us how long the clear skies will last!

Evening red and morning gray, two sure signs of one fine day.
Usually true. Dew and low-lying fog, or mist, makes everything look soft and gray. Like dew, fog may appear after a cloudless night when the ground is cool. The water droplets soon evaporate when the warmth of the sun heats the air.

When the mist creeps up the hill,
fishers, it's time to try your skill.
Usually true. Mist rises when there is warm air and sunshine, so it's a perfect time to go fishing.

No weather is ill if the wind be still.
Not always true! While this saying is often true in the summer, you may also have heard people warn about "the calm before the storm."

If woolly fleeces are in the sky, be sure the day is fine and dry.
True. Woolly fleeces, like sheep? Yes! Cumulus clouds look like big fluffy sheep. These clouds are also known as "good weather" clouds because they are usually accompanied by sunshine.

When ladybugs swarm, expect a day that's warm.
True. Ladybugs will only fly in warm weather and become very active when they get too hot. They collect heat under their shells and release it by flying.

When the wind is from the West, then the fishes bite the best.
Somewhat true (in temperate zones). Western winds bring the fairest weather, so it may be the nicest time to be out in a boat. Another version of this saying goes, "The wind in the West suits everyone best."

Yellow streaks in a sunset sky, wind and daylong rain are nigh.
True. Cirrus clouds look like "yellow streaks" at sunset. The Latin name for these clouds mean wispy hair, which is just what they look like. These clouds are a sign of changing weather. "Nigh" in this saying means coming soon.

Frogs will call before the rain, but in the sun are quiet again.
Questionable. While animal behaviors can be observed, they are hard to prove scientifically. One explanation for hearing loud croaks before the rain? The croaks sound louder because sound travels better in humid air.

Whether it's cold or whether it's hot,
we shall have weather, whether or not.
True! This we can depend on. Weather is always changing, from day to day
and throughout the year. The air that surrounds our earth is always being heated
or cooled, resulting in wind, clouds and precipitation (such as rain, hail, snow
and sleet).

Ring around the moon, rain will come soon.
Usually true. A halo (or ring) around the moon appears when there are
cirrostratus clouds, which are very high clouds made of ice crystals. They
are a sign that the weather is changing and there might be rain coming.

Red sky in the morning, sailors take warning!
True (in temperate zones). If you see a red sky in the morning, it means calm
air has already passed over you and stormy weather will be coming. Red clouds
aren't a great sign either. They mean you likely have a low-pressure system
already overhead. If you are a sailor, prepare for a storm or head to shore!

Trout jump high when rain is nigh.
True. When there is low air pressure, it usually spells rain. Before the rain
comes, insects fly low, looking for cover. Minnows, on the other hand, come
to the surface of the water, following the rising gas bubbles that have been
released by the low air pressure. If you are out before the rain, you might see
fish jumping to catch the low-flying insects or in pursuit of the minnows.

Hear the whistle of the rain? 'Tis a sign it's going to rain.
True. Sound travels better through air with high humidity. When there is
moist air and cloud cover, the sound waves travel along the surface of the
water or ground instead of scattering upwards.

Winds of the daytime wrestle and fight,
longer and stronger than those of the night.
True (except behind a cold front). At night the air is cool, but when the sun
heats the air in the daytime, warm and cool air mix, creating wind.

Wind from the East is neither good for man nor beast.
True (in temperate zones). In places like North America or Europe, where
winds usually move from west to east, eastern winds bring cold and storms.
Animals can sense a change in the air pressure before storms arrive. Some
people can, too, complaining of aches and pains in their joints.

Little ships must keep to shore. Larger ships may venture more.
True. Little ships are advised to make their way to a safe port when there are
warning signs of an approaching storm. Large ships are more stable in rough
waters.

If seabirds fly to land, there truly is a storm at hand.
True. Seabirds are very sensitive to changes in temperature and air pressure.
By instinct they know when a storm is approaching. The sea can be quite
nasty when the weather turns, so seabirds will come to shore to seek shelter.

When clouds appear like rocks and towers,
the Earth is refreshed with frequent showers.
True. High, towering clouds are called cumulonimbus clouds. Their name
means heaping storm clouds in Latin. If these clouds darken and you hear
thunder, head for cover!

Cats leap about and chase their tails
to warn of thunderstorms and gales.
True. While cats aren't great weather forecasters, sailors used to watch their
behavior closely. Have you ever had your ears pop? Your ears are adjusting to
a change in air pressure. Cats are much more sensitive and have been seen to
act nervously and hide when the air pressure drops. Sailors took this strange
behavior as a sign of a coming storm.

When the forest murmurs and the mountains roar,
close the windows and shut the doors!
True. Sound travels better before a storm. If you hear the sound of wind in the
distance, prepare for a storm.

The more rain, the more rest. Fair weather's not always best.
True. When these sayings were common, the rain was a welcome rest for the
many people who used to work outside, often from sunrise to sundown.

Elly MacKay is an acclaimed paper artist and children's book
author and illustrator. She wrote and illustrated the picture
books *If You Hold a Seed*, *Shadow Chasers* and *Butterfly Park*,
among others. Elly's art was also featured on the covers of
Tundra Books' reissues of L. M. Montgomery's Anne of Green
Gables and Emily of New Moon series. Her distinctive pieces
are made using paper and ink, and then are set into a miniature
theater and photographed, giving them their unique three-
dimensional quality. A member of the Cloud Appreciation
Society, Elly lives in Owen Sound, Ontario, where she watches
the weather with her husband and two children.